Welcome

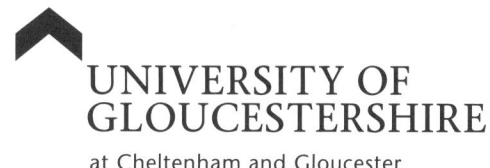

UNIVERSITY OF GLOUCESTERSHIRE
at Cheltenham and Gloucester

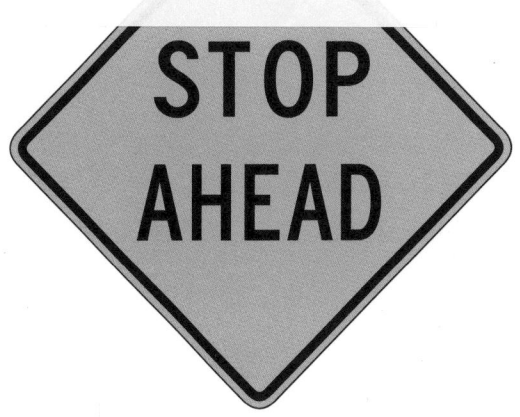

An AVA Book

Published by AVA Publishing SA
Chemin de la Joliette 2
Case Postale 96, 1000 Lausanne, Switzerland
Tel: +41 786 005 109
Email: enquiries@avabooks.ch

Distributed by Thames and Hudson
(ex-North America)
181a High Holborn, London WC1V 7QX
United Kingdom
Tel: +44 20 7845 5000
Fax: +44 20 7845 5055
Email: sales@thameshudson.co.uk
www.thamesandhudson.com

Distributed by Sterling Publishing Co., Inc.
in the USA
387 Park Avenue South
New York
NY 10016-8810
Tel: +1 212 532 7160
Fax: +1 212 213 2495
www.sterlingpub.com

in Canada
Sterling Publishing
c/o Canadian Manda Group
One Atlantic Avenue
Suite 105, Toronto
Ontario M6K 3E7

Copyright © AVA Publishing SA 2005

ISBN 2-88479-049-7
10 9 8 7 6 5 4 3 2 1

English Language Support Office
AVA Publishing (UK) Ltd.
Tel: +44 1903 204 455
Email: enquiries@avabooks.co.uk

Design and text by Russell Bestley and Ian Noble
Original photography by Sarah Dryden

Production and separations by AVA Book
Production Pte. Ltd., Singapore
Tel: +65 6334 8173 Fax: +65 6334 0752
Email: production@avabooks.com.sg

VISUAL RESEARCH

AN INTRODUCTION TO RESEARCH METHODOLOGIES IN GRAPHIC DESIGN

IAN NOBLE
RUSSELL BESTLEY

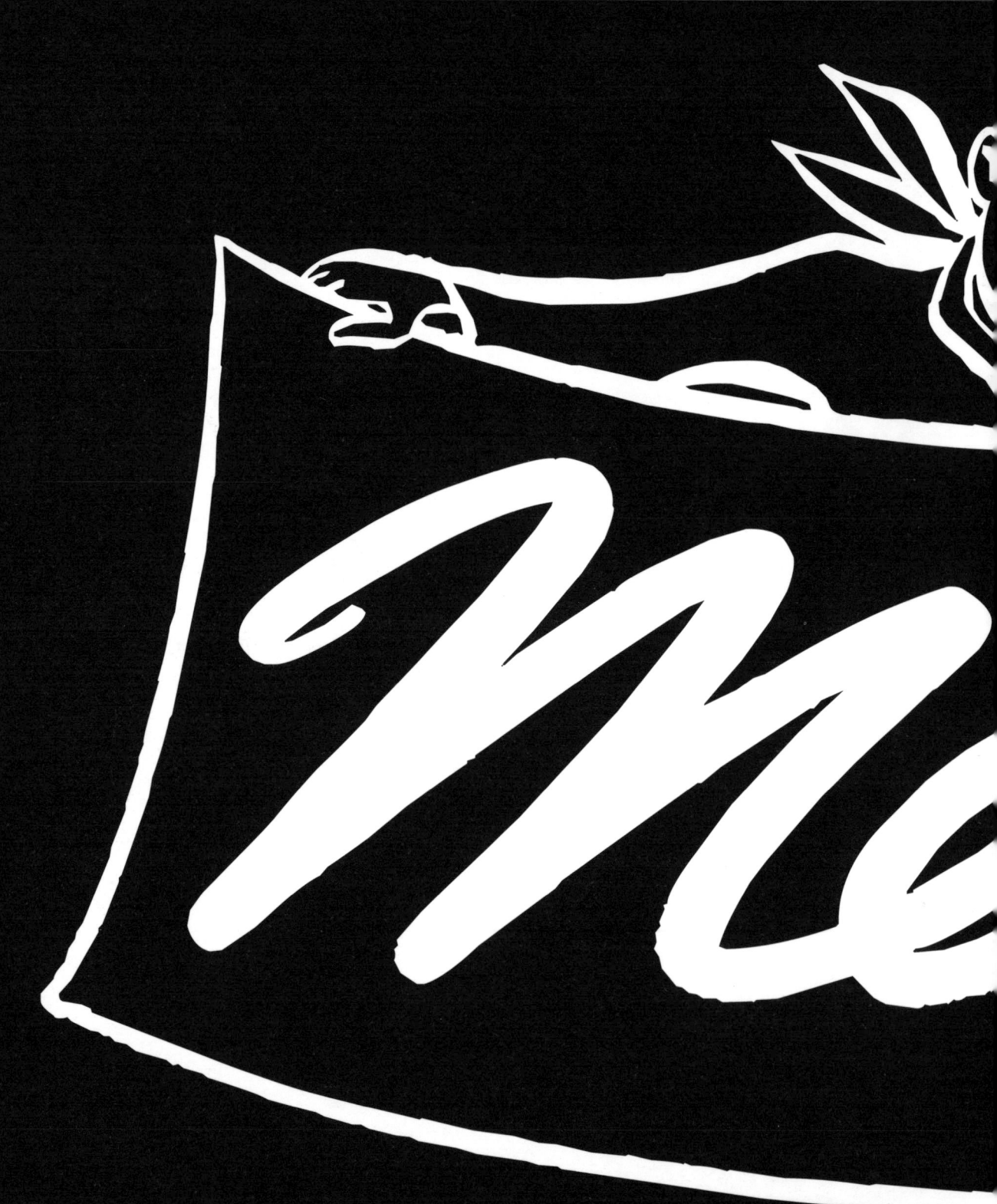

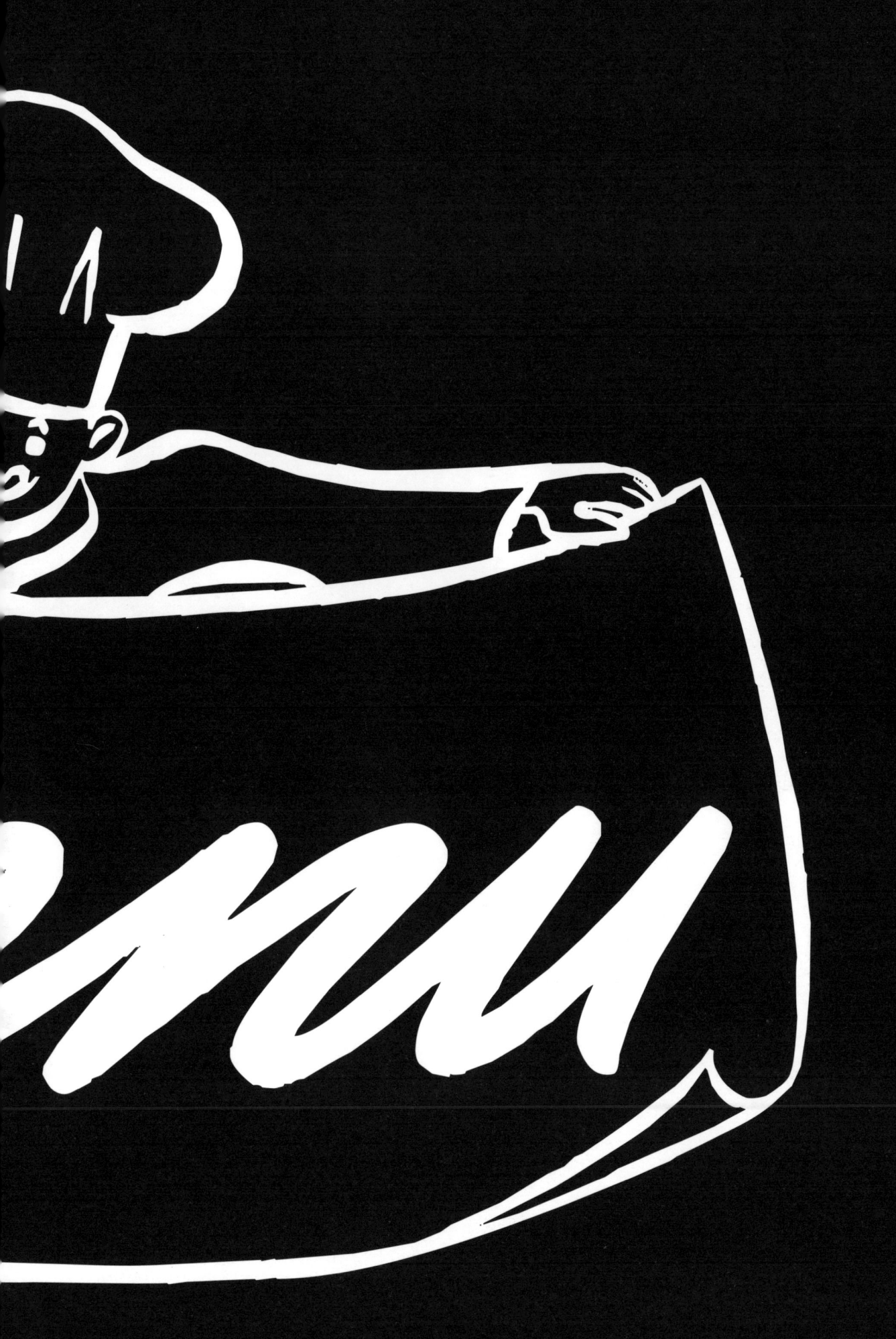

1/2

Contents

3/4

Contents

5/6

Contents

This book is designed to lead the reader through a wide range of research methodologies, incorporating a central text reflecting the key arguments and theoretical propositions together with visual examples of work by professional practitioners and postgraduate students. Individual sections of the book deal with analysis of existing work and the development of practical skills and visual research methods with which to create new work. Chapters are each given a core emphasis, but also cross-reference to other sections that directly relate to the topics explored.

Thematic spreads throughout the book are designed to operate as individual units, carrying both the main text relating to core subjects and a range of additional information specific to the work featured as examples and illustrations. Case studies incorporate detailed image captions relating to the featured work, together with background information on the context and brief.

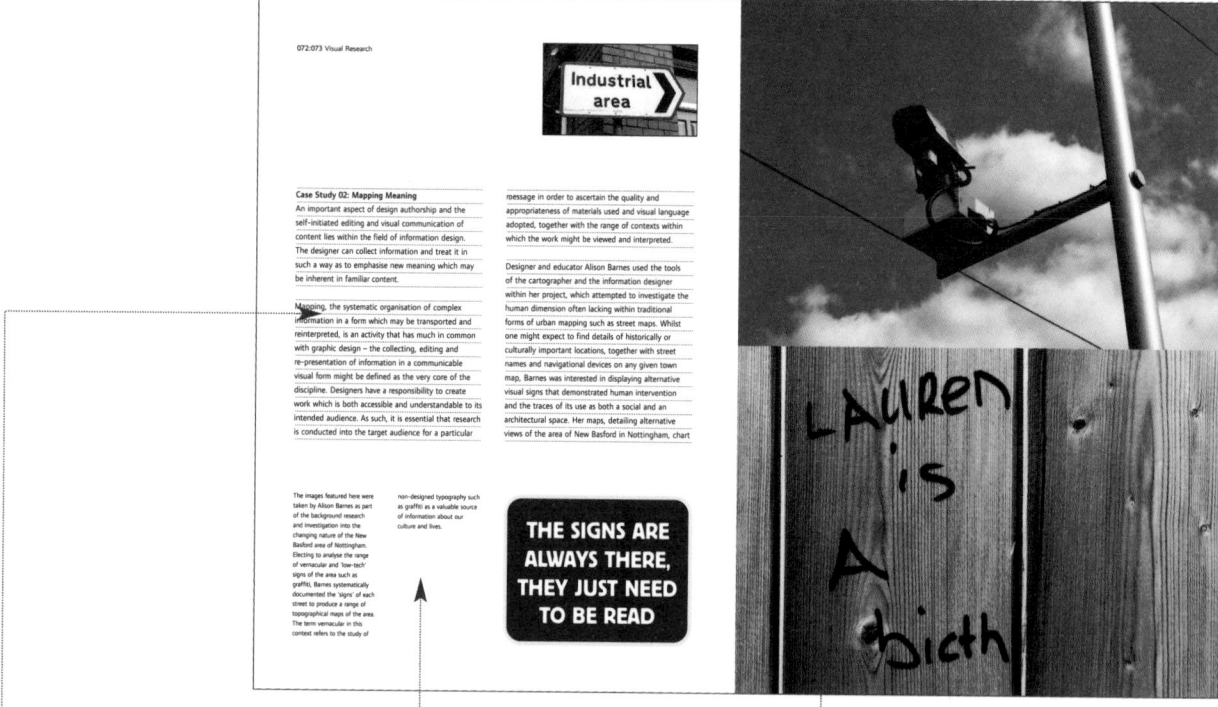

★ **Main Text:** The central description of chapter themes, outlining the key theories and practical methods for each section.

★ **Image Caption:** Caption information for images and illustrations used on the spread.

★ **Images:** Examples of design projects, both professional and self-initiated, which help to illustrate and support theories put forward in the main text.

How To Get The Most Out Of This Book

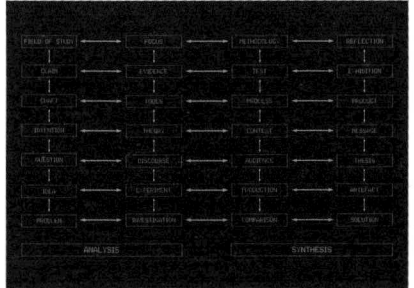
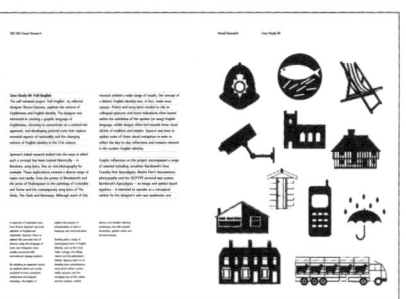
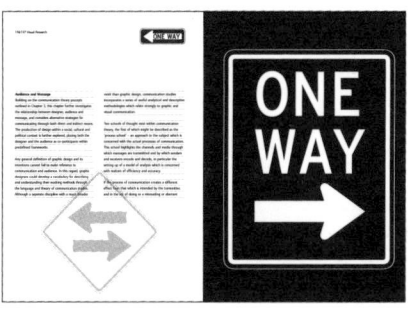

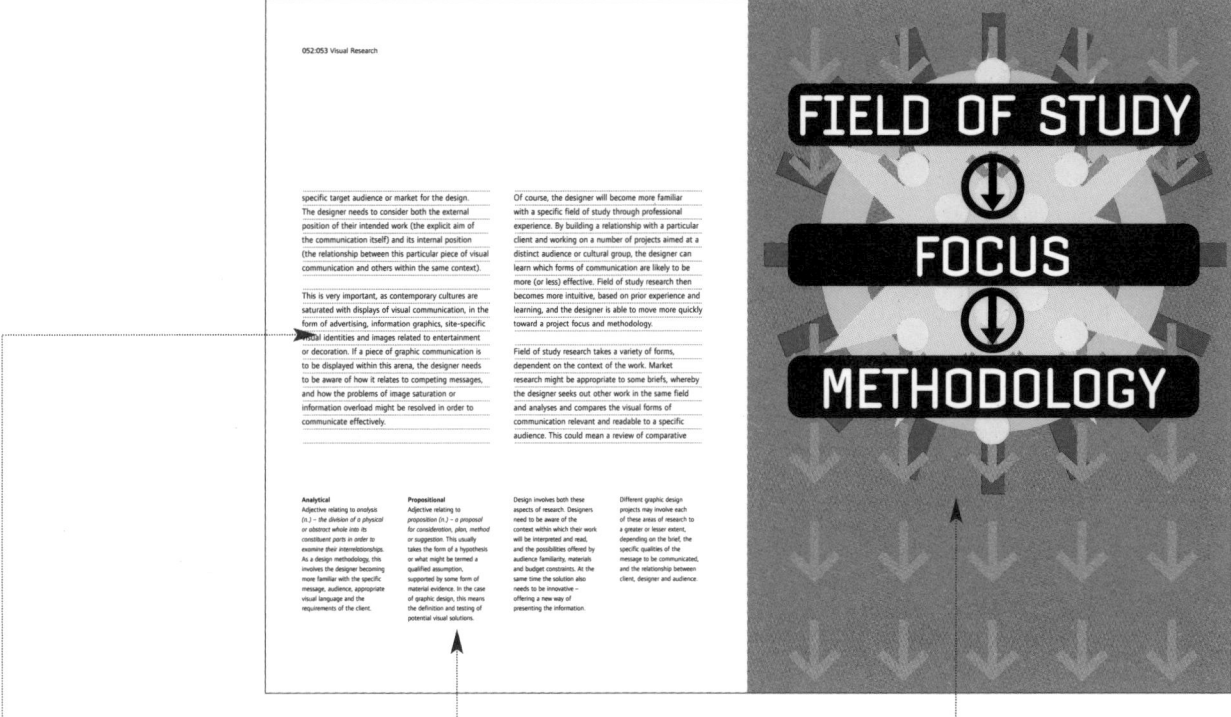

★ **Main Text:** The central description of chapter themes, outlining the key theories and practical methods for each section.

★ **Further Information:** Definitions of terms used in main text, further references and links to other chapters.

★ **Illustrations:** Accompany main text in order to visualise the key themes explored.

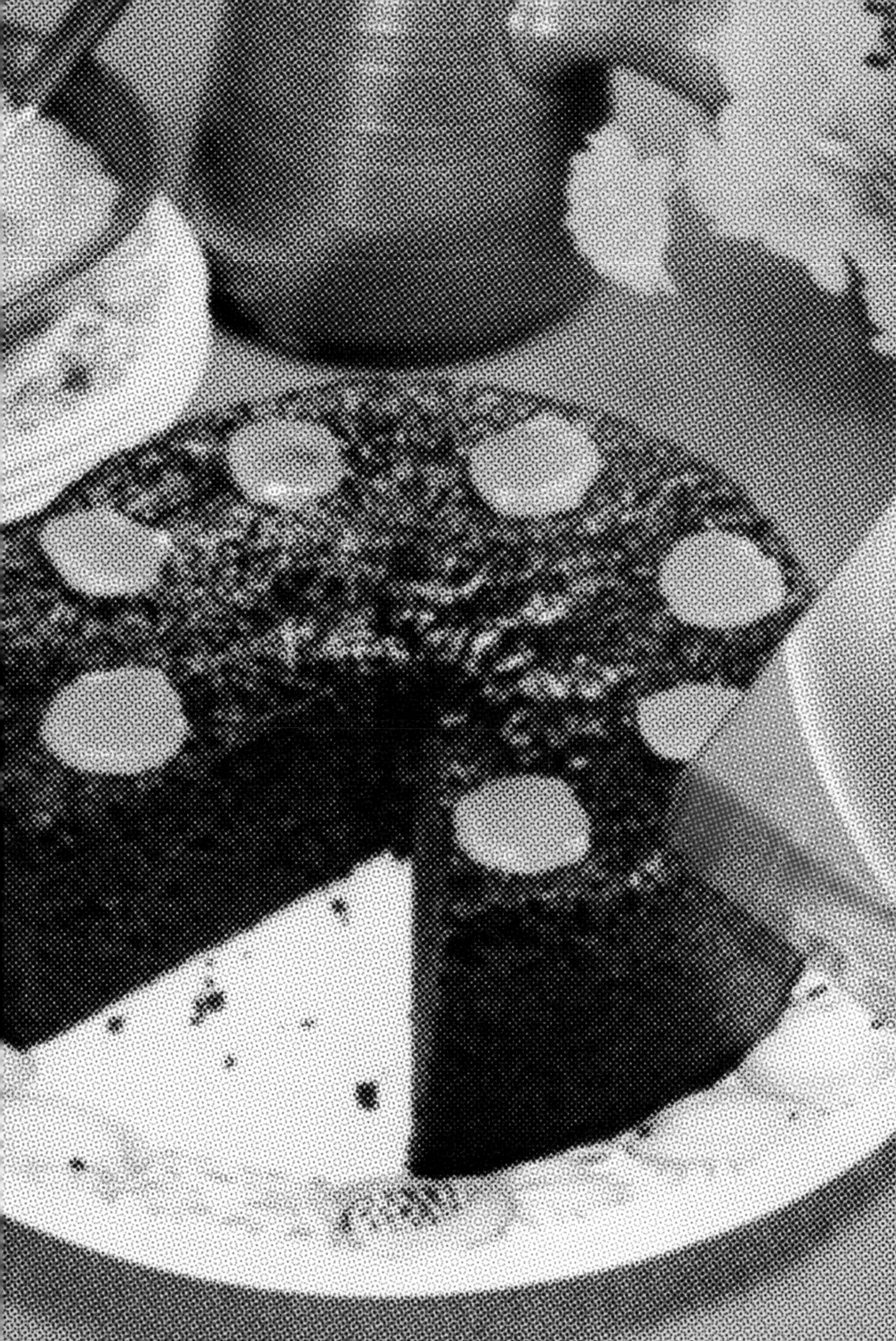